#1412-L

Red 5

Int 7-8

2 9/4 ea

Henry 568

Man rules now where once the dinosaur was king.

"Dinosaurs dominated the world for 120 million years. . ."

DIGGING FOR DINOSAURS

EDWIN H. COLBERT
Chairman, Geology and Paleontology
Curator of Fossil Reptiles and Amphibians
and
WILLIAM A. BURNS
Editor, Man and Nature Publications
The American Museum of Natural History

Illustrations by Robert Borja

j 568

CHILDRENS PRESS, Chicago

PICTURE ACKNOWLEDGMENTS

The full color photographs and illustrations in *Digging For Dinosaurs* are the work of the
following photographers and artists, whose collaboration is gratefully acknowledged. For the full
color pictures, American Museum of Natural History (1, 15, 17, 19, 20, 22, 25, 27, 28, 29, 30, 32):
Orville Goldner (2, 3, 4, 5, 6, 7, 8, 9, 10, 11, 12, 23); I. Howard Spivak (13, 14, 16, 18, 21, 24, 26,
31). Designed by Robert Borja. Front matter illustrations by Robert Borja. We also thank
Dr. Theodore White and the staff of Dinosaur National Monument for their cooperation in the
preparation of this book.

CONTENTS

THE DINOSAUR'S FAMILY TREE

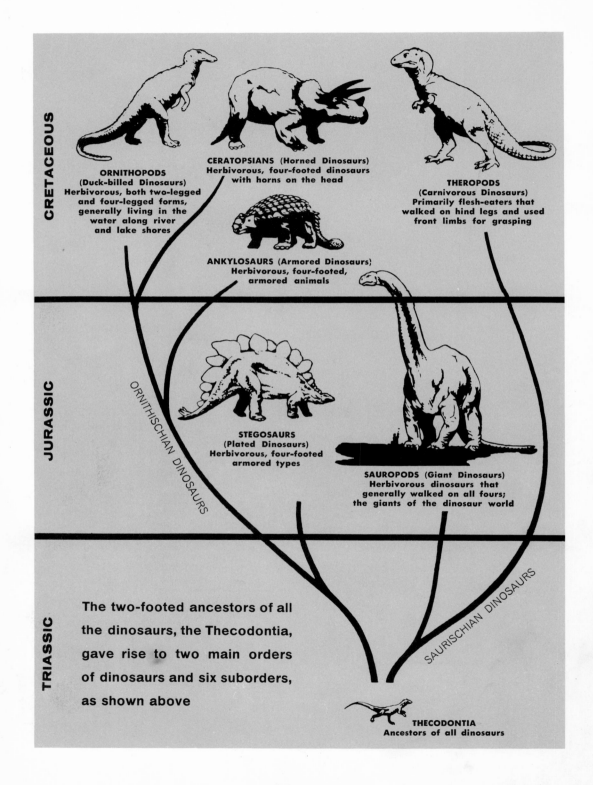

CRETACEOUS

ORNITHOPODS
(Duck-billed Dinosaurs)
Herbivorous, both two-legged
and four-legged forms,
generally living in the
water along river
and lake shores

CERATOPSIANS (Horned Dinosaurs)
Herbivorous, four-footed dinosaurs
with horns on the head

THEROPODS
(Carnivorous Dinosaurs)
Primarily flesh-eaters that
walked on hind legs and used
front limbs for grasping

ANKYLOSAURS (Armored Dinosaurs)
Herbivorous, four-footed,
armored animals

JURASSIC

ORNITHISCHIAN DINOSAURS

STEGOSAURS
(Plated Dinosaurs)
Herbivorous, four-footed
armored types

SAUROPODS (Giant Dinosaurs)
Herbivorous dinosaurs that
generally walked on all fours;
the giants of the dinosaur world

TRIASSIC

The two-footed ancestors of all
the dinosaurs, the Thecodontia,
gave rise to two main orders
of dinosaurs and six suborders,
as shown above

SAURISCHIAN DINOSAURS

THECODONTIA
Ancestors of all dinosaurs

8

SOME EARLY AMPHIBIANS AND REPTILES

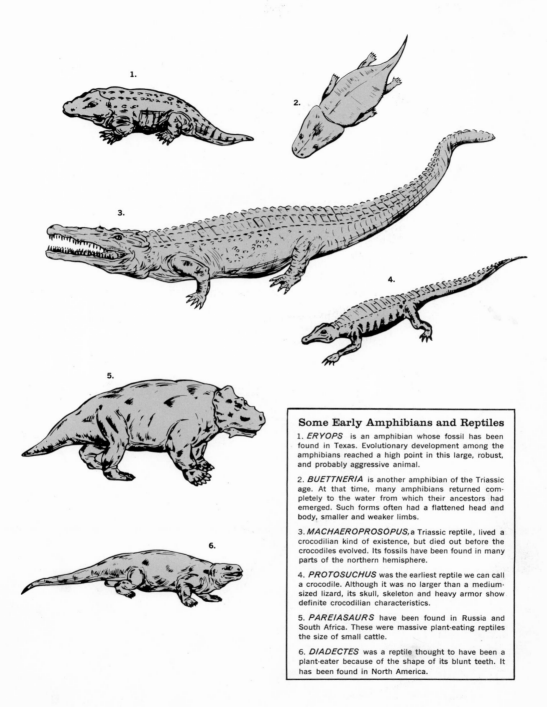

1.

2.

3.

4.

5.

6.

Some Early Amphibians and Reptiles

1. *ERYOPS* is an amphibian whose fossil has been found in Texas. Evolutionary development among the amphibians reached a high point in this large, robust, and probably aggressive animal.

2. *BUETTNERIA* is another amphibian of the Triassic age. At that time, many amphibians returned completely to the water from which their ancestors had emerged. Such forms often had a flattened head and body, smaller and weaker limbs.

3. *MACHAEROPROSOPUS,* a Triassic reptile, lived a crocodilian kind of existence, but died out before the crocodiles evolved. Its fossils have been found in many parts of the northern hemisphere.

4. *PROTOSUCHUS* was the earliest reptile we can call a crocodile. Although it was no larger than a medium-sized lizard, its skull, skeleton and heavy armor show definite crocodilian characteristics.

5. *PAREIASAURS* have been found in Russia and South Africa. These were massive plant-eating reptiles the size of small cattle.

6. *DIADECTES* was a reptile thought to have been a plant-eater because of the shape of its blunt teeth. It has been found in North America.

DIGGING FOR DINOSAURS

THE STORY OF LIFE ON EARTH IS PERHAPS THE MOST
fascinating known to man. Life extends so far back in time that
the story is shrouded in mystery. Within the past hundred
years, however, man, with his unending curiosity and thirst for
knowledge, has been able to uncover many of nature's deeply
hidden secrets.

Those who have done the most to discover the earth's history
are called geologists (scientists who study the structure of the
earth) and paleontologists (scientists who study the life of the
past). They are the "detectives" of natural history who work
entirely from clues and evidence left millions and millions of
years ago in the many levels of the earth's crust. One of the
most amazing stories they tell is about those terrifying creatures
known as dinosaurs (DINE-*o-sawrs*).

Dinosaurs were an ancient group of reptiles. They were cold-
blooded animals. Like today's crocodiles, lizards and snakes
their blood temperature was the same as the air or water that
surrounded them. They could not survive if it was too hot or
too cold.

Dinosaurs were supreme rulers of the earth for about 120 million years. Some dinosaurs grew to fantastic size, weighing as
much as 40 tons; others were quite small, no larger than a little
dog. Some dinosaurs were vegetarians or plant-eaters. Others
were carnivores or flesh-eaters, who preyed on the plant-eaters.
Some lived in the water or in swamps, others on dry land. A
close relative of the dinosaurs, the *Pteranodon,* was the first
animal with a backbone (vertebrate) to fly.

Of all the creatures that lived in ancient times, dinosaurs seem
to hold the most fascination. We meet them in comic strips, in
books, and in fantastic motion pictures. Some people like to

believe that dinosaurs still exist in remote, unexplored areas of the world, but this is not true. No man, living or dead, ever met a live dinosaur. Dinosaurs appeared upon the earth about 200 million years ago, and were extinct millions of years before the first man appeared.

This book tells the story of dinosaurs and of the paleontologists and geologists whose work has re-created the earth's history through aeons of time. Here you can go on a scientific expedition to search for the past and see reconstructions or restorations of how the wonderful and awesome dinosaurs may have looked as they roamed the earth. But first you must learn more about the earth itself.

Skeleton and Restoration of the Thecodont Reptile

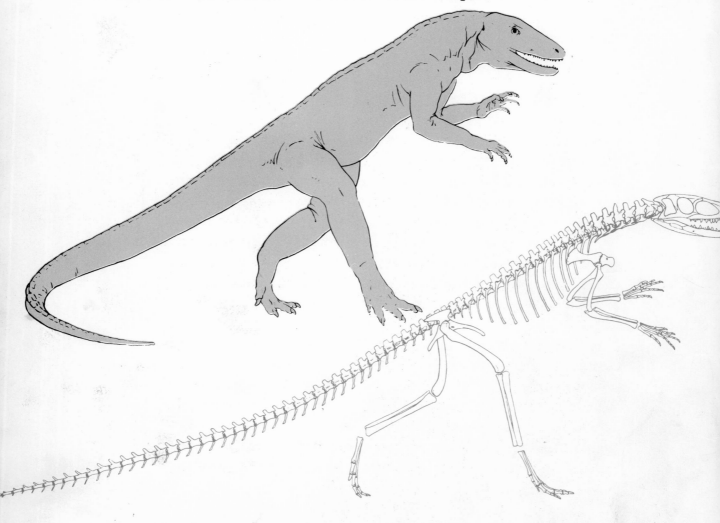

HOW THE EARTH BEGAN

No one knows exactly how the solar system began. Scientists have several theories that help to explain the probable origin of the sun and the planets. Most scientists agree that the sun is the parent of all the other planets in our solar system. Yet at first only a mass of hot gases and dust swirled through space. This mass gradually changed. The center became the sun. The outer rings continued to move rapidly around the sun gathering more gases, cosmic materials and dust. They grew. Eventually, as they cooled, these rings developed into the nine planets—Mercury, Venus, Earth, Mars, Jupiter, Saturn, Uranus, Neptune and Pluto.

Most scientists believe that the sun was formed billions of years ago, although the planets themselves came into being much later. By measuring alterations of certain radioactive minerals in the earth's crust, scientists can determine how long the earth has existed. They have estimated that the earth began about four or five billion years ago!

Scientists now agree that at first the earth, as well as the other planets, was a fiery mass of gas and dust. As time passed these gases cooled and thickened into a red-hot liquid sphere. As the cooling process continued, this liquid ball slowly developed a rocky crust. The heavier molten metals sank to the center giving the earth low and high areas. Rain fell, rising back to the heavens again as steam. Finally the rocky crust became quite cool and the rain collected in pools and lakes, spilling over the uneven surface to form rivers. Masses of granite rock, lighter than the metals, were pushed up to form great continents, and seas were formed. As rain continued to fall, rivers flowed and sediment from the crumbling rocks was washed into the sea to harden into layers of new rock. This process is still going on today.

In these layers of sedimentary rocks, one upon the other, geologists find their clues to the earth's ancient past. In them, too, paleontologists find fossils. Fossils are the remains or evidence of prehistoric plants or animals. A fossil may be a bone, a shell, or a rock imprint of a tiny plant or animal. It is the study of these ancient remains that allows the geologist and the paleontologist to reconstruct the prehistoric past so vividly. Through

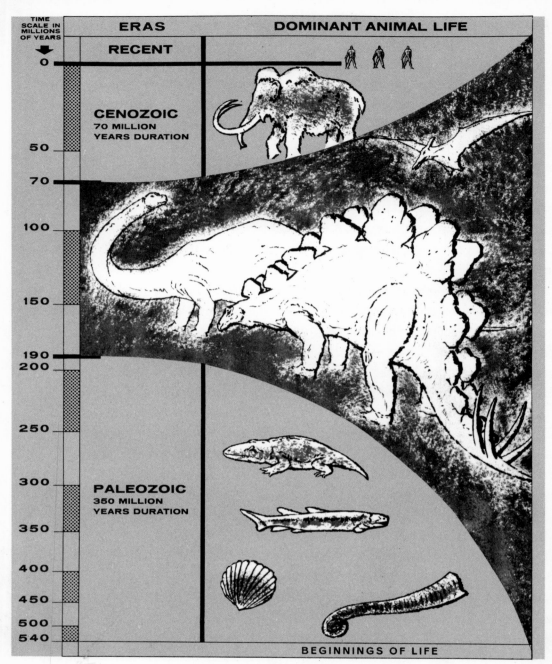

TIME SCALE IN MILLIONS OF YEARS	ERAS	DOMINANT ANIMAL LIFE

Geological Time Chart

their study of fossils and the earth, geologists have been able
to develop a geological calendar. This calendar divides the
earth's history into several chapters, known as eras. It sub-
divides each era into lesser units of time called periods. These

eras and periods of geologic time serve as guide in following the development of varied prehistoric and historic plants and animals. This time guide gives sequence to the earth's history.

Each era is marked by many changes in the earth's surface. Mountains rise, then erode away; seas shift; volcanoes erupt. The record of each event is written in the rocks for the geologists to read. A seashell or ancient fish fossil found on the plains in Kansas, for example, proves to us that this area was once under the sea. With each change in the earth's surface—and it has been forever changing—there have been changes in climate, which often altered forms of life. The plants and animals that could adjust to changing conditions survived. Those that could not died.

Although the earth is about four or five billion years old, life has existed upon it only during the last 500 million years. Our Geological Time Chart shows three eras—Paleozoic (*pale-ee-uh-ZO-ik*), Mesozoic (*mess-uh-ZO-ik*), and Cenozoic (*see-nuh-ZO-ik*). These three eras are those that cover the time through which scientist detectives have traced fossil remains of life on earth.

The Beginning of Life

Scientists agree that earliest forms of life appeared in the sea. The first living things must have been tiny, one-celled organisms, like the protozoa we know today, so soft that they could not become fossilized. During hundreds of millions of years these one-celled organisms reproduced themselves, evolving into different forms. Both plant and animal life became abundant in the water—not only in the sea but also in rivers and lakes. Seaweed, sponges, bacteria and other plants and animals evolved. From this type of life developed shelled invertebrates, or animals without backbones. Finally during the Paleozoic era, more than five million years ago, the fish appeared. The fish were the first animals with backbones. These vertebrate fish were the forerunners of all vertebrates to follow—amphibians, reptiles, birds, mammals.

Through aeons of time, seas continued to advance and recede; rivers flowed across the land. Finally, conditions became favorable for some plant and animal life to leave the water for the land. Vertebrates who could breathe without the use of gills evolved. These were the amphibians, descended from fresh-water fish. From amphibians came the primitive reptiles, ancestors of the dinosaurs.

This progression of life took about 350 million years. Finally the Mesozoic era, known as the Age of Reptiles, began. This era has been divided into three great periods lasting a total of about 120 million years—Triassic *(try-ASS-ik),* Jurassic *(joo-RASS-ik)* and Cretaceous *(kree-TAY-shuss).* Triassic comes from a word meaning "group of three," since the rocks from this period, first studied in Germany, were found to be deposited in three distinct layers. The Jurassic period was named after the Jura Mountains in Europe where the rocks from this age were first studied. Cretaceous comes from a Latin word meaning "chalk." Such names have become a part of the universal scientific language and are used throughout the world to identify rocks formed in one of the periods of the Mesozoic era, whether they are found in the Jura Mountains or in your own backyard.

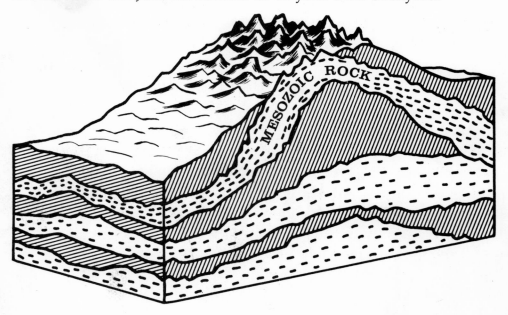

This cross-section of the earth's layers shows how violent movements and erosion have combined to bring Mesozoic rocks to the surface.

The Dinosaurs

When scientists search for dinosaur fossils, they must find rock formations of these three periods, deposited when dinosaurs were widespread throughout the world.

Dinosaurs did not appear suddenly. These reptiles had their origins during the Triassic period. At this time the climate was warm and moist, just right for cold-blooded reptiles, great and small, and for the vegetation upon which many of them fed. Fish swam in the seas, lakes and rivers. Creatures without backbones continued to multiply on land and sea; many different kinds of insects were present, too. But by the time of the Jurassic and Triassic periods, dinosaurs were dominant over all other creatures on earth.

"Dinosaur" means "terrible lizard." There were two distinct orders of reptiles—the saurischian *(saw-RIS-kee-an)* dinosaurs and ornithischian *(or-ni-THIS-kee-an)* dinosaurs. Saurischian means "reptile-hipped," and in these dinosaurs the three bones of the hip are arranged more or less according to the typical reptilian plan. The ornithischian or "bird-hipped" had hip bones arranged somewhat as in the pelvis of birds.

Originally, all the saurischian dinosaurs were meat-eaters. The fierce killers, like *Allosaurus (al-low-SAWR-us),* "Leaping

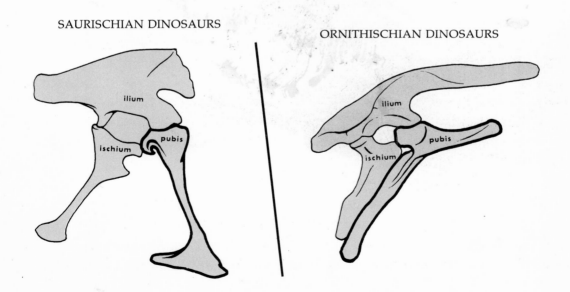

SAURISCHIAN DINOSAURS

ORNITHISCHIAN DINOSAURS

17

Lizard," and *Tyrannosaurus rex (ti-ran-o-SAWR-us* REKS) or "King Tyrant Lizard," belonged to this order. From some meat-eating dinosaurs, the great plant-eaters, like *Brontosaurus (bron-toe-SAWR-us)* or "Thunder Lizard," evolved. The ornithischian dinosaurs—such as *Triceratops,* "Three Horned Face Lizard"— were plant-eaters exclusively and they were more numerous than the fierce carnivores, or flesh-eaters.

During the late Cretaceous period, roughly 70 million years ago, dinosaurs were present throughout all continental areas of the earth except Antarctica. Then, sometime during the transition from the Cretaceous to the Paleocene *(PALE-ee-o-seen)* period of the Cenozoic era, the dinosaurs disappeared. They became extinct.

Why? There is no certain answer. Climatic conditions were becoming more harsh. It was colder. Plant life was changing; the dinosaurs may not have been able to adapt to a changing world. All we know is that these great reptiles died out rather suddenly, in the geological-time sense. The small, furry, warm-blooded mammals, which during the age of the dinosaurs were so unimportant, became the inheritors of the earth.

The Science of Paleontology

Before we go looking for dinosaur remains, let's first learn something about paleontology, the science that deals with past life. Baron George Cuvier, a French anatomist, is regarded as the father of vertebrate paleontology because he was the first to make a comprehensive scientific study of backboned fossils. Dr. Gideon Mantell, an Englishman who wrote the first description of a dinosaur, spent much of his life digging for and studying these ancient reptiles. Sir Richard Owen, first director of the Natural History division of the British Museum, coined the word *Dinosauria.*

Adults were not the only people digging for fossils. A little girl, Mary Anning, who lived on the south coast of England, helped her father collect fossil seashells which were sold to vacationers. She never found a giant dinosaur bone but she did discover the first skeleton of a seagoing fossil reptile, *Ichthyo-saurus (ik-thee-o-SAWR-us)* "fish-lizard," in 1811 when she was twelve years old. In 1821 she made another great find—the *Plesiosaurus (plee-see-o-SAWR-us),* a reptile thoroughly adapted to life in the ocean. Seven years later she found the skeleton of a flying reptile, a pterosaur (TER-*o-sawr*) "wing-lizard," one of the first to be discovered in England.

The first dinosaur to be found in the United States was un-covered by workmen. Dr. Joseph Leidy, the man who gave vertebrate paleontology its start in America, identified this find as the *Trachodon,* "duck-billed" dinosaur, so called be-cause of its flattened skull.

Many other Americans pioneered in the study of fossils, but two men stand out—Othniel Charles Marsh and Edward Drinker Cope. Instead of waiting for fossil bones to be uncovered by accident these two men formed expeditions and searched for them. Friends at first, they later became bitter enemies and fought over their fossil finds like two dogs over a bone. Science won the final battle, however, because their competition created great collections which are among the world's finest. Much of Cope's collection can be seen at the American Museum of Natural History in New York City; Marsh's is on display in the Peabody Museum at Yale University.

Today, scientists exchange information and ideas, each worker contributing his part to man's knowledge of the past. Geology and paleontology, as well as other natural sciences, are taught in universities throughout the world. This is as it should be, because it is now evident that all life, past and present, is related.

A long yesterday ago, in terms of geologic time, a fish-like animal crawled out of the water and reproduced its kind upon the land, starting a new cycle of life on the earth. From this crea-ture has come the amazing multiplicity of life which resulted in dinosaurs and other forms. The story of the dinosaurs is one of great proportions, stretching over long periods of the earth's history. Their reign is so vast that it dwarfs man's time on earth almost to insignificance.

130 MILLION YEARS AGO

This is a painting of a Mesozoic landscape as scientists have reason to believe it looked at the time of the dinosaurs. Perhaps the very spot where you live was once much the same. Where your familiar trees now grow on a gentle hillside, giant tree ferns, horsetails and gingko trees might have flourished. In this primitive swamp giant dinosaurs freely roamed, feeding off the prehistoric plant and animal life.

In this picture you see two giant meat-eating allosaurs (AL-low-saurs), saurischian (lizard-hipped) dinosaurs, looking for their next meal. Allosaurs walked on their hind legs. Their weight was supported by their strong back legs and mighty tail. Their small claw-like front legs and long, sharp teeth were perfect for grasping and tearing apart their victims. The allosaurs were indeed fierce meat-eaters.

Partly hidden by the trees we can see three camptosaurs (CAMP-toe-saurs). These dinosaurs were among the first of the ornithischian (bird-hipped) dinosaurs. They could walk on all fours or on their back legs. These plant-eaters were not equipped to fight. Without a doubt the camptosaurs made many fine meals for the allosaurs.

The two huge reptiles with the double rows of plates on their backs are stegosaurs (STEG-oh-sawrs). Their armored backs and spiked tails were their protection. No one attacked them without a fight and just possibly some memorable battle scars. The stegosaurs were plant-eaters.

And there far out in the water are the gigantic brontosaurs (BRON-toe-saurs) or thunder lizards. The brontosaur was also a lizard-hipped dinosaur. But unlike its cousin, the allosaur, it was a plant-eater. Brontosaurs supported their massive weight—sometimes as much as 35 tons—on four stout legs. Brontosaurs spent much of their time in the water using the water's buoyancy to support their weight. Water also protected the brontosaurs from their meat-eating enemy—the allosaur.

The long, snake-like neck of the brontosaurs was topped by a very tiny head which was home to an even tinier brain. It probably didn't weigh more than a pound.

These are only a few of the prehistoric dinosaurs, but before we meet them individually let's join a scientific expedition. We will go on a fossil hunt. Our objective is to *find a dinosaur*.

THE LAND TODAY

Today there may be only eroded rock, sand, desert plants and little water where once ancient plants grew luxuriantly in steaming swamps. These rocks were formed millions of years ago. Throughout this vast area are rock layers that date back to the Mesozoic era, the Age of Reptiles. In them, if we are lucky, we'll find a dinosaur.

Fossils are found in sedimentary rocks—sandstone, limestone, shale; sometimes in coal, asphalt, and even in amber and other materials. Erosion—the action of wind and waves, and hundreds of thousands of years of rainfall—wears away great masses of rock. When a bone hunter finds a place where erosion is just uncovering a specimen he is lucky. He knows that he has located a spot where conditions were right for fossilization and that other specimens are nearby.

Erosion is the paleontologist's greatest helper. Without it the dinosaur remains for which we are now searching might be buried forever—far down in the earth.

PALEONTOLOGIST AT WORK

The noted paleontologist Dr. Theodore White, of Dinosaur National Monument near Vernal, Utah, examines part of the upper jaw of a meat-eating dinosaur. We will learn from men like Dr. White where to look for the kind of rock in which dinosaurs can be found, how to recognize fossils when we find them, and how to safely take specimens out of their ancient beds.

A hundred years or so ago, there were few paleontologists. The science was just beginning. There were no handbooks to tell you how to dig up, prepare or study fossils. When a workman found a strange bone or two while digging the foundation for a house, or while quarrying stone, he might take it to the nearest professor for identification. Perhaps the bones passed from hand to hand until they ended up in a "cabinet," as early museums were called. Today we have experts to help us.

So let's head for the western United States where many dinosaur fossils have been found. It's time for our expedition to begin.

A FIELD EXPEDITION

This is fossil country. It is a rough and rugged land. There are no modern conveniences here. From now on our group will be living in the open.

Some of us have brought cots or air mattresses for sleeping on the ground. All of us have sleeping bags to protect us from the cold nights. Our supplies include all the food, tools and extra clothing we'll need to survive in this open country.

The most important thing brought along, however, is the knowledge carried in the minds of our scientific experts. They are experienced in many phases of the natural sciences—zoology and biology—but they are specialists in the fields of geology and vertebrate paleontology. By watching these scientists at work we will learn where to look for a dinosaur, how to recover it from the rocks, and how to preserve and ship it safely to the museum laboratory.

FOSSIL-BEARING ROCK

Sometimes, if the bone hunter is extremely fortunate, he may find fossils exposed by weathering. This picture shows part of the fossil backbone of a prehistoric creature partially uncovered by erosion.

A fossil is the remains or indications of an organism that lived in a past geologic period. There are all kinds of fossils — reptiles, birds, insects, mammals, plants, and one-celled creatures so tiny that we must search for them with a microscope.

How are fossils formed? A fish, a dinosaur, or a fern died in some past era and was covered by mud or sand. As the organic matter slowly decayed, it was replaced by mineral matter that later turned into stone.

Fossils are found in the sedimentary rocks that were formed after the animal died. Men who work in stone quarries often turn up fossils. Sometimes fossils appear on the face of an eroding cliff. A trained paleontologist, however, never searches in a hit-or-miss fashion. He goes where there are rock formations that contain the type of fossil he seeks.

"WALKING OUT" FOSSIL BEDS

We are seeking a dinosaur. We must, therefore, find rock layers that were formed during the Mesozoic era, the time when dinosaurs were living upon the earth.

Our geologists have found an outcropping of Mesozoic rock that shows evidence of fossils. We'll "walk it out" to find how the rocks lie, then follow them wherever they may lead us.

Finding dinosaur-bearing rocks is not a simple matter of digging in the earth until you come to the right layer, as you would if you wanted to find water under sand. The crust of the earth has been, and still is, subject to tremendous pressures that are great enough to force up huge land masses, mountains and cliffs. Thus, ancient layers of rock may be thrust up through layers of newer rock. You must know your geology to tell one from the other.

If you could look beneath the top layers of the earth's crust, you would observe many varieties of rock layers, or strata. Some are smooth and straight; others are rolled like ocean waves. Some are horizontal; others are tilted at sharp angles.

LOOKING FOR EVIDENCE

We follow our horizon of Mesozoic rock along cliff faces, as this scientist is doing—down arroyos and washes, up mountains, through canyons—always looking for evidence that fossils are present. It is hard, grueling and sometimes discouraging work.

This level we are walking out in our search for fossils was formed during the Mesozoic portion of earth's history. Rock strata do not usually occur in straight, regular layers. Great earth movements and upheavals may shift the original layers so that it is very difficult to follow them. Mesozoic rock, in which dinosaur fossils are found, must first be located and the extent of its exposure determined.

So we climb on, looking in every direction.

WE FIND A SPECIMEN

Finally we find what we are looking for—a specimen! We are no longer thirsty. Hunger has gone. Fatigue has passed. After days of barked shins, sunburned necks and backs, strained eyes, we find this grayish-brown spot that doesn't look quite like the other rock around it. We investigate with our pick, and uncover a fragment of fossil bone.

Leaving our pick to mark our find, we go back to camp to tell the others. Hard work is about to begin.

First, the rock that covers the fossil must be removed. This rock is called the "overburden" and may weigh many tons. Working day after day in the hot sun, the outlines of the skeleton are gradually exposed. Then, using tools as fine as those used by jewelers, the rock next to the bone is carefully scraped away, and the fine dust brushed out with whisk brooms. All exposed bones and teeth are quickly covered with rice paper and shellac to protect them from the elements. Fossils are very delicate once they are exposed to the air. The slightest slip of a pick might shatter them.

WORKING ON THE SPECIMEN

Specimen after specimen is uncovered as we dig deeper. Here in this lonely spot, millions upon millions of years ago, conditions were just right for fossilization.

After the overburden has been removed, the bones are uncovered carefully with pick, hammer, chisel, awl and brush. Now the extent of the skeleton can be judged. The skeleton is removed from its ancient bed, bone by bone. If this is not possible, blocks of rock containing several bones are cut out.

Paleontologists may go to the trouble of removing several tons of overburden, sometimes with blasting techniques as well as pick and shovel, only to find that the fossil disappears within a few feet. (When they are very lucky, they may find skeletons on open flats with little or no overburden!) When they have removed the individual bones additional steps must be taken to protect them. If a sudden desert rainstorm should blow up while the men are working, they will have to cover their work quickly with a tarpaulin to protect the delicate bones from the water.

PLASTERING THE SPECIMEN

At this point, the paleontologists begin to prepare the specimens for safe shipment to the museum laboratory.

Many specimens are removed from their ancient beds still encased in large blocks of rock, later to be delicately removed in the laboratory. Shellac is applied to such blocks to seal and protect them in transit.

When individual fossil bones are uncovered in the field, additional steps must be taken to protect them. In the same way that a doctor puts a plaster cast around a broken bone, strips of rough burlap are cut from a roll, dipped in a plaster-of-paris mixture, and wrapped in layers around the specimen. If the bone is quite large, splints are included in the bandage wrapping to give it greater strength.

Day after day fossilized bones are removed from this newly discovered site. Excitement is running high. There can't be the slightest doubt now. Enough bones have been uncovered to tell the scientists that they have found the remains of a mighty dinosaur.

EXCAVATING THE SKELETON

It is *Brontosaurus,* one of the largest creatures to walk the earth, a plant-eater that belonged to the saurischian order of dinosaurs. It lived in or near the water, its only protection from the meat-eating *Allosaurus.* It seems hard to believe that water and abundant plant life once covered this arid spot.

Here is just one of the huge bones of our brontosaur. Compare its size with the size of the man working on it. This dinosaur was truly a mighty giant which, more than 100 million years ago, walked the earth during the Jurassic period. One of its bones may weigh hundreds of pounds, and some of them are well over six feet long.

As "earth detectives," we've been quite successful. We came to find a dinosaur and we've found one of the very largest of them all. It has been hard work. Now that the work is over, we have blisters and calluses to prove it. But it was worth it, for when the skeleton has been reassembled and placed on display in the museum, thousands of people will stare at its mighty frame and marvel that creatures such as this once roamed the earth.

THE MUSEUM LABORATORY

This man is working on a fossil that has been sent to the museum laboratory from the field. Once the dinosaur fossils have arrived, the parts embedded in blocks of stone or encased in plaster, a great deal of work remains to be done. The burlap and plaster must be removed. Other bones must be carefully taken from the rock in which they are embedded. Each bone is carefully cleaned, then shellacked again to harden it. The larger bones are drilled, and steel rods are inserted to support them for mounting.

When every part of the skeleton is prepared, the paleontologist, with the help of his staff of preparators and technicians, puts these puzzles of the ancient past back together again.

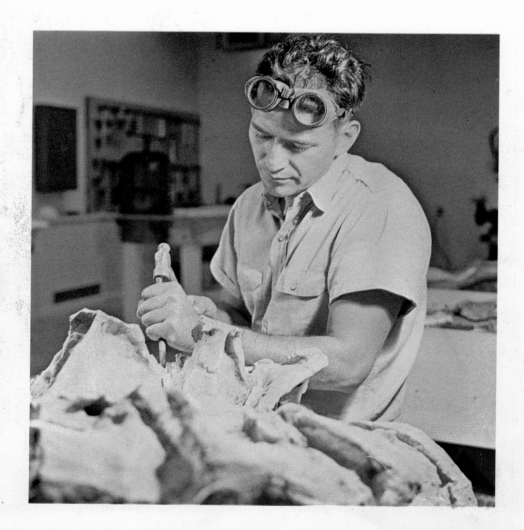

THE BRONTOSAUR SKELETON

Here is the completed mounting of a huge brontosaur, on display at the American Museum of Natural History in New York City.

Brontosaurus is typical of a suborder of saurischian dinosaurs known as sauropods ("lizard-foot"). These giant plant-eating dinosaurs lived during the late Jurassic and Cretaceous times. Most of them walked on all fours. They had extremely long necks and tails but very small heads. This skeleton of *Brontosaurus* is some 67 feet long and is 15 feet high at the hips. The living animal probably weighed about 35 tons, seven times more than a large African elephant.

SKELETON OF A DIMETRODON

Now that we know something about our dinosaur *Bronto-saurus*, let's find out about other fossil reptiles. Some people get the impression that dinosaurs were the only prehistoric reptiles. But there were many others that lived long before the dinosaurs came along. The one whose skeleton we see here is called dimetrodon *(dye-*MET*-ro-don)*.

Dimetrodons belonged to a large group called the pelycosaurs (PEL-*i-ko-sawrs*). Pelycosaur means "basin lizard," and the name was applied because of the basin-shaped pelvis of the animal. The pelycosaurs began as long reptiles with sinuous bodies and sprawling limbs, somewhat resembling lizards (which, however, didn't appear until millions of years later). We know about them from fossils found mainly in the red shale and sandstone beds of Texas and adjacent states.

Although many of the pelycosaurs were not much larger than today's lizards, some attained fairly good size. One of these large pelycosaurs was this seven-foot-long dimetrodon.

RESTORATION OF A DIMETRODON

This is a painting of a restoration of a dimetrodon done by a famous museum artist, the late Charles R. Knight. Here we can see the tremendously long spines on the backbone that supported its "sail." Perhaps the most logical explanation of the sail is that the cold-blooded dimetrodon required a temperature-regulating device, a large "radiator" to provide a cooling surface if the weather was too hot, or a sun-absorbing surface if the weather was too cold. This is only one of many theories as to the function of dimetrodon's sail.

Some people thought that the sail served to protect the dimetrodon from enemies, but we know that there were no other large meat-eating reptiles living at that time which could have preyed on the dimetrodon. Another theory is that the sail was not functional but the result of an unbalanced growth that did not seriously interfere with the survival of the animal. Even if we are not sure of the purpose of this sail, it must have been clumsy for the dimetrodon to carry around and it must also have been a drain on the blood supply and energy of the animal.

THE ALLOSAUR SKELETON

Many of the world's greatest dinosaur fossils are to be found in the western part of the United States. This great meat-eating *Allosaurus* of the Jurassic period was found in Como Bluff, Wyoming.

The *Allosaurus* had hands (as its forefeet are called) armed with hook-like claws made for gripping its prey. It was some 35 feet long, and it must have been a fearsome sight as it stalked across the land in search of its food. We know that it was two-legged — that is, it walked and ran on its powerful hind legs. How fast it could go we do not know. It must have been able to run fast enough to catch up with almost any of the other creatures on which it was accustomed to feed. Because of its bulk and the construction of its hind feet, the allosaur more than likely restricted its hunting to the dry land between lakes and swamps, catching unwary plant-eaters before they could escape to the safety of swampy ground.

With its great size and formidable equipment, the *Allosaurus* did not have to fear any other prehistoric creature. Like the *Tyrannosaurus rex*, which came along millions of years later, it was the ruling reptile of its own period, the Jurassic. It is shown here tearing at the backbone of a brontosaur — and if you were actually standing close enough, you could find teeth marks on the brontosaur backbone, marks which might have been made by the bite of an allosaur.

Sometimes the paleontologist also makes a painted restoration to show how an animal of ancient times lived, what it ate, and how it might have looked in its actual surroundings. This next painting of a restoration shows the fierce meat-eater *Allosaurus*, now clothed in flesh and in its natural habitat.

ALLOSAUR RESTORATION

Although the allosaur was not as large as the fiercest of the meat-eaters, *Tyrannosaurus rex,* it was still an awesome beast. The sharp, dagger-like teeth cut with a slicing action, and when its mouth was closed, the sharp teeth of the lower jaw sheared past the upper teeth. In this way, the *Allosaurus* was able to cut and tear sizable chunks from its unfortunate victims, such as the *Brontosaurus.*

SKELETON OF A STEGOSAUR

This skeleton of *Stegosaurus*, the so-called "plated" dinosaur, was discovered in Bone Cabin Quarry, Medicine Bow, Wyoming. The stegosaurs were walking fortresses—huge animals protected by thick skin, carrying a deadly four-spiked weapon in their tail, and wearing an arrangement of upright, triangular plates down their back. *Stegosaurus* must have had few enemies because almost any meat-eating animal would have found it difficult to find a good place to make an attack.

This was an ornithischian (bird-hipped) dinosaur that walked on all fours. Its front legs were much shorter than its hind legs, giving the animal a high, arching curve to its back.

STEGOSAUR RESTORATION

This picture shows you a restoration of a *Stegosaurus*. Although it was a plant-eater this creature was certainly frightening to behold. The average stegosaur was about 20 feet long and about nine feet tall at the hip. Its small head was carried close to the ground. Four stout legs supported a weight that ranged from seven to ten tons.

Here was an animal three times as large as an elephant, but with a brain no bigger than a walnut. The brain of this huge, lumbering beast was actually twenty times smaller than an enlargement of the spinal cord in the hip, which helped to control the movements of its hind legs and dangerous tail.

Its most formidable offensive weapon was its tail. If any other animal came too close, the stegosaur only had to swing its powerful tail to punch four holes at a time in the hide of its enemy. The plate arrangment on its back may also have served as a protection for the spinal column.

Stegosaurus presumably lived in the uplands or higher ground between the swamps and marshes. Like other plant-eaters its teeth were weak. It could probably only eat soft, lush vegetation. It protected itself from the attacks of *Allosaurus* by its thick hide, heavy plates, and a viciously swinging tail.

It is believed the stegosaur appeared first in the Jurassic period. But as far as scientists have been able to determine they were extinct early in the Cretaceous period.

However, plated dinosaurs did not die out completely when the stegosaur did. Another type developed. This was the *Ankylosaurus*. This creature was smaller but more heavily protected than its ancestor. The ankylosaur lived during the Cretaceous period.

GEORGE J.
GESELSCHAP
1942

THE TRACHODONS

Now we jump ahead about 60 million years to see what kinds of dinosaurs were then living. The period we have arrived in now—the Cretaceous—might be called the "Twilight of the Dinosaurs," for it was at the end of the Cretaceous period that dinosaurs finally disappeared from the face of the earth.

In this period we find the interesting *Trachodons* (TRAY-*ko-dons*), or *Anatosaurs*. This creature's skull was flattened, particularly in front, to form the broad "duck bill" that makes it so easy to recognize them.

The trachodons were plant-eaters and found their food among water plants in the shallows of rivers and lakes. They also lived along the seaside. Perhaps they ate a few mollusks from time to time. When they were threatened by enemies, they were ready to dash into the water to protect themselves, somewhat in the manner of *Brontosaurus*.

The anatosaur or trachodon walked on strong, broad three-toed feet. Their feet were not clawed. They were more like rounded hoofs. Their four fingered forelimbs were much shorter than the hind legs. But the way they were constructed leads scientists to believe that apparently the trachodon occasionally walked on all fours.

From the evidence left by the trachodon it is believed to have been a very good swimmer. The remains of the forelimbs show that webs of skin were present between its fingers. Similar webs may also have been present on its hind legs.

The trachodon's mighty tail was also suited for swimming. Scientists believe it was used in the side-to-side movement employed by present-day alligators and crocodiles.

THE PROTOCERATOPS

The horned dinosaur *Protoceratops (pro-to-*SER-*a-tops)* was not particularly large nor is it thought to have been very ferocious. But it is one of the most famous of the dinosaurs because skeletons of it were found with its fossilized eggs on an expedition of the American Museum of Natural History into Outer Mongolia, conducted by the museum's former director, Dr. Roy Chapman Andrews. This dinosaur, *Protoceratops andrewsi,* was named after Dr. Andrews.

This little dinosaur grew to a maximum length of about five or six feet and walked on all fours, not on its hind legs as did some of the other dinosaurs. All the horned dinosaurs, big or small, were characterized by the development of the front of the skull into a large, pointed beak, and the back of the skull into a wide, flaring frill that extended over the shoulders. The frill of *Protoceratops* was very small in the newborn dinosaur but grew larger as the animal matured.

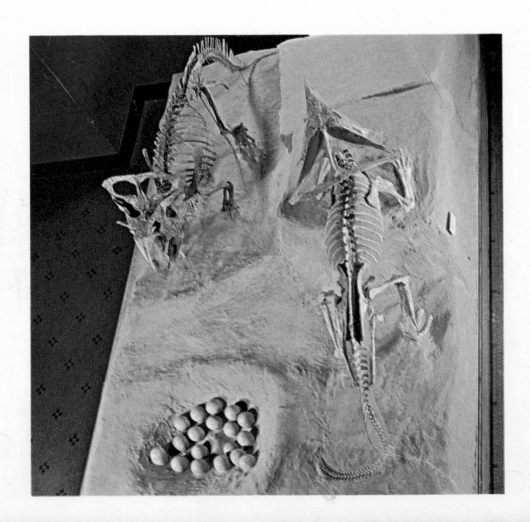

DINOSAUR EGGS

Here are some dinosaur eggs found by the Outer Mongolia expedition of the American Museum. This is how they were discovered: Dr. Walter Granger of the museum brought in part of an eggshell which the scientists thought at first to be that of a fossil bird. Later, one of the members of the party came back to camp saying that he had found some dinosaur eggs. No one believed him; however, the scientists went to see what he had found. There they were—three eggs, partly broken, beside a sandstone ledge. The brown shells of the fossils looked so much like modern eggs that there could be no mistake. All the loose egg fragments were carefully collected and a large part of the sandstone ledge was cut out and sent back to the American Museum. The scientists found thirteen more eggs at this spot, just as they had been left by the dinosaur when she laid them millions of years ago. Some of the eggs had unhatched dinosaurs preserved in them.

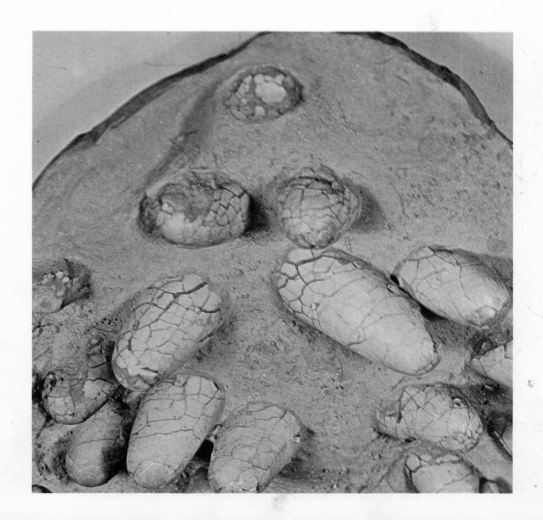

RESTORATION OF BABY DINOSAURS

This restoration shows the baby *Protoceratops* dinosaurs just coming out of their eggshells after hatching. Although there is no scientific evidence, the Protoceratop must have been ready to fend for itself from the moment it left the egg, since reptiles are not noted for taking care of their young.

The expedition that went into Outer Mongolia was a combination motor and camel caravan. Camels carried the heavy supplies and gasoline. The motor cars were thus able to go far ahead of the caravan, waiting for it to catch up when supplies were needed.

When the scientists returned to the American Museum, they brought back 60 cases of specimens weighing five tons. They had collected 70 skulls, 14 skeletons and more than 70 dinosaur eggs.

THE TRICERATOPS

Now let's look at a relative of our little *Protoceratops,* the great three-horned *Triceratops (try-SER-a-tops). Triceratops* evolved from the modest beginnings exemplified by *Protocera-tops.* Of all the horned dinosaurs, *Triceratops* is perhaps the best known. The picture shows a mounted skeleton of this huge animal, with its dangerous-looking horns and great flaring collar. Compare the size of the dinosaur with the size of the young lady.

Triceratops was from twenty to thirty feet long. It probably weighed about ten tons. It stood some eight feet high at the hips. It walked, like all the horned dinosaurs, on short, broad feet. Four sturdy legs supported its massive weight.

Its most remarkable feature was its enormous head, which actually made up fully one-third of the entire length of its body. It had a hooked, parrot-like beak, a stout horn on its nose and a long, sharp horn over each eye. It must have been a formidable opponent when defending itself.

RESTORATION OF TRICERATOPS

The sculptured restoration of *Triceratops* shows us much more. Now we can observe, in profile, the great skull, the heavy, hooked beak, the three deadly horns, and the flaring frill that reached over the creature's neck and shoulders. The bony frill must also have been a mighty shield to protect *Triceratops*, to some extent, from attack by other animals.

The great skull of this beast was fastened to its backbone by an ingenious ball-and-socket joint. The skull was balanced upon this joint and controlled with the tremendous neck muscles attached to the bottom of the frill. With this great head and the strong leg muscles, *Triceratops* must have had a remarkable ability to hook with its horns and to make short, powerful lunges with its head down. The two horns over the eyes, when directed forward, could be used to impale any enemy that might approach within striking distance. Such defenses must have been very useful to the three-horned dinosaur, for it lived in a land inhabited by *Tyrannosaurus rex*, largest of the meat-eating dinosaurs.

TYRANNOSAUR RESTORATION

Evolving from a line of smaller but awe-inspiring meat-eating dinosaurs, *Tyrannosaurus rex,* the "king of the dinosaurs," was the greatest and most fearsome land-living carnivore that the world has ever known. It was an animal of magnificent proportions and terrible power. Modern lions, tigers or bears appear to be almost dwarfs by comparison.

This giant among meat-eaters was wonderfully put together for destructive purposes. Its legs were exceptionally strong and it had a stout pelvis between its backbone and limbs that acted as a lever. Its forelegs were much smaller than its mighty hind legs.

This painting of *Tyrannosaurus rex* shows this most awesome of beasts as it possibly looked in life.

THE KING OF THE DINOSAURS

The giant *Tyrannosaurus*, standing on its powerful hind legs, carried its head about eighteen or twenty feet above the ground. It was about as tall as a two-story house. The distance from the tip of the nose to the tip of the tail was fifty feet. It probably weighed some eight or ten tons.

Because of its tremendous size and upright posture, *Tyrannosaurus* was equipped with heavy, strong legs. Its feet were broad, forming a good support and furnishing traction against the ground. Unlike the brontosaur, it was able to move swiftly on its two powerful hind legs, which carried sharp claws. But the forelimbs of the *Tyrannosaurus rex* were relatively small and it must have had little use for them. They were more like arms.

The four-foot skull of *Tyrannosaurus* was a tremendous structure, powerfully built, with a mouth of great size. The teeth, some almost six-inches long and one-inch wide, were like curved daggers.

In attacking other dinosaurs for food, it used a combination of the terrible claws and dagger-like teeth. Its size and dominance over the other animals of its time led to its scientific name: *Tyrannos* (tyrant) — *sauros* (lizard) — *rex* (king) — or "king of the tyrant lizards."

Thus far, we have seen certain prehistoric reptiles that walked on the ground, namely the dinosaurs and a pelycosaur that lived earlier than the dinosaurs. Let's now turn our attention to early flying creatures. In Jurassic times, when *Brontosaurus* made its appearance, two groups of backboned animals ventured into the air to soar on outstretched wings.

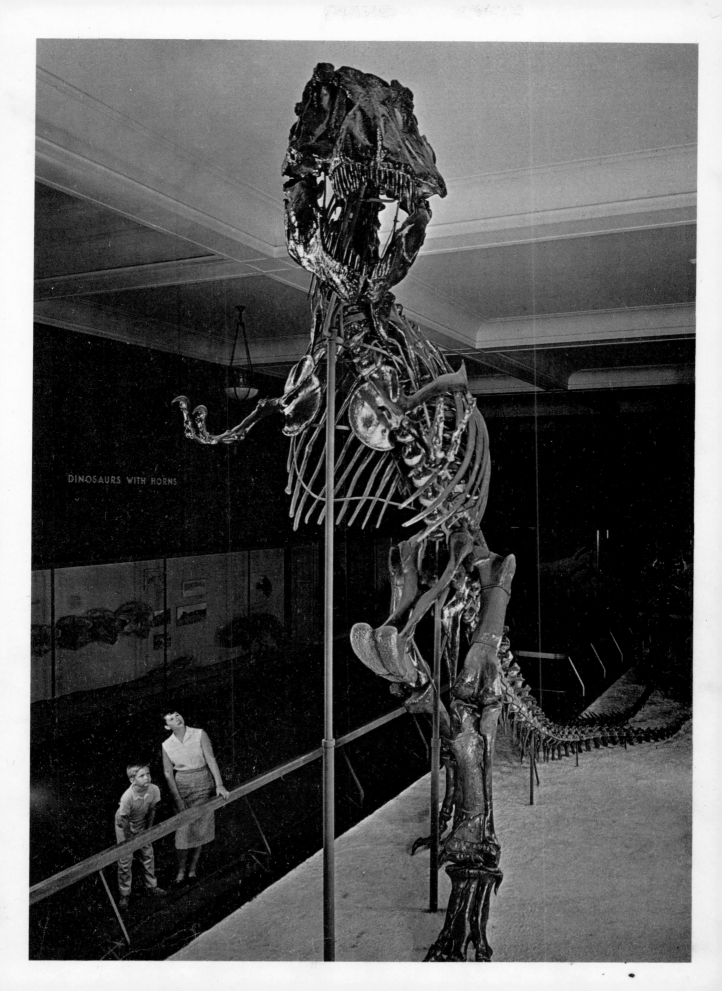

DINOSAURS WITH HORNS

RESTORATION OF PTERANODON

Both of these groups were closely related to the dinosaurs. One group developed warm blood, wings and feathers, thus becoming birds. The other group, the pterosaurs, which could fly, remained reptiles.

If a backboned animal is to fly, it must develop along the following lines: the front limbs must become wings. The bones must be very light but strong and the muscles powerful. The nervous system must be highly developed and the sense of balance very precise. All these things were accomplished by the early vertebrate fliers.

Some of the flying reptiles of the Jurassic period were rather small, often no larger than sparrows or robins. But some Cretaceous flying reptiles—70 to 120 million years ago—were giants among nature's flying machines. The pterosaur shown in this picture is *Pteranodon (ter-RAN-o-don),* a flying reptile with a maximum wingspread of about twenty-seven feet!

The flying reptiles more than likely glided and soared as much as they flew. They were lightly built, and even the giant *Pteranodon,* with its enormous wingspread, had a relatively small body.

SKELETON OF ARCHAEOPTERYX

The pterosaurs were not the ancestors of our modern birds. The discovery of the earliest birds came about as an indirect result of the printing industry. Some of the world's finest lithographic limestone used for printing comes from Bavaria, Germany, and workmen there, cutting out blocks of it many years ago, uncovered a very imperfect skeleton. Study showed that this was a perching bird, vastly more primitive than any type now in existence.

A few years later, a nearly perfect specimen was found also in Germany. This picture shows you a reproduction of such a skeleton cast in plaster. The original is now in the British Museum of Natural History, but casts were made of this important discovery and distributed all over the world.

It seemed to the bone hunters who studied the skeleton that the creature must have fallen to the bottom of a shallow lagoon, where it was covered with mud deposit. The mud gradually turned to stone, preserving the bones of *Archaeopteryx (ar-kee-OP-ter-ix)*.

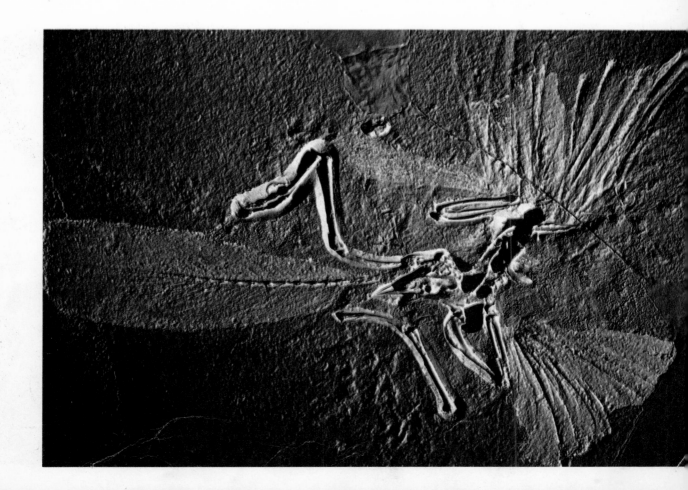

RESTORATION OF ARCHAEOPTERYX

Archaeopteryx was a most remarkable creature and might be termed a "missing link" in the evolution of birds. But it would be more accurate to call it a "connecting link," since the birds and the reptilian pterosaurs were derived from the same common ancestor.

The wing of the crow-sized *Archaeopteryx* was a rather primitive structure. In modern birds, the first three "fingers" or digits of the wing are joined to form a strong base for the flight feathers. But in our prehistoric bird, the second and third digits extended beyond the flight feathers. Each digit ended in a claw which was possibly used for climbing or for holding onto steep, rocky surfaces. It may have been that when *Archaeopteryx* was shedding its feathers and could not fly, it used the wing-hooks to climb about.

Archaeopteryx had some bird-like features, such as hollow bones and feathers, and some very pronounced reptilian features as well, such as teeth. This picture clearly shows the long reptilian tail with feathers arranged on either side of it.

A FOOTPRINT DETECTIVE STORY

In the American Museum of Natural History is evidence of one of the world's most ancient mysteries.

In the Brontosaur Hall are six forefoot and six hindfoot impressions made by a huge brontosaur as it tramped through mud which ages ago hardened into limestone. With these larger tracks are smaller three-toed tracks. What do they mean? We know that the smaller tracks belonged to an allosaur that lived at the same time and preyed upon the huge brontosaur.

Here is what may have happened. The brontosaur perhaps was feeding in the marsh when the allosaur saw it and attacked. The brontosaur took to the open water, leaving great footprints behind. The smaller dinosaur followed, stepping into some of the larger tracks. We know that there must have been some water over the mud through which the brontosaur walked, because there were no tail tracks. The tail probably was supported by the water.

The unsolved mystery is this: did the allosaur catch his meal, or did the brontosaur reach safety in the water? No one knows.

BRONTOSAUR RESTORATION

This is our final picture—a restoration of our brontosaur as it might have appeared in life, its long, snakelike neck raised high above the marsh grasses, perhaps looking for an approaching enemy. We've learned about this ancient creature while finding and piecing together its bones left in solid rock. We've also learned much about other kinds of ancient reptiles that lived millions upon millions of years ago.

The sauropod dinosaurs, huge though they were, are not the largest or heaviest animals found in the world. The great blue whales reach lengths up to 100 feet, and weights up to 130 tons. They, however, are buoyed up by water. The sauropod dinosaurs probably do represent the maximum size that can be reached by land animals, where bones, muscles and ligaments must support the body against the constant downward pull of gravity.

Fossils of *Brontosaurus* and its relatives have been found in South America, Africa, Asia, Australia, North America, and Europe. This gives us a good indication of how widespread and dominant these giant dinosaurs were during Mesozoic times.

Our expedition into the prehistoric past has now come to an end. We might think that the dinosaurs, because they are extinct, were failures. But this is not so. They were the dominant creatures on earth for over one hundred million years. Man rules now where once the dinosaur was king. But man has ruled only about a million years. Mankind has millions of years to go before the record of the dinosaurs can be matched.

PLACES TO VISIT

Here is a list of museums where you can see mounted dinosaur skeletons.

THE AMERICAN MUSEUM OF NATURAL HISTORY, Central Park West at 79th Street, New York, N. Y. One of the world's greatest collections of dinosaurs, including *Brontosaurus, Tyrannosaurus, Stegosaurus, Triceratops,* numerous other horned dinosaurs, duck-billed dinosaurs, armored dinosaurs, and others described in DIGGING FOR DINOSAURS.

UNITED STATES NATIONAL MUSEUM, Washington, D.C. Notable display of dinosaurs, especially *Diplodocus, Stegosaurus,* and others.

PEABODY MUSEUM OF YALE UNIVERSITY, New Haven, Conn. Noted for the fine display of dinosaurs in its collection.

ACADEMY OF NATURAL SCIENCES, Philadelphia, Pa. A skeleton of *Corythosaurus,* a duck-billed dinosaur.

AMHERST COLLEGE MUSEUM, Amherst, Mass. Mounted skeleton of the duck-billed dinosaur, *Trachodon.*

NATIONAL MUSEUM OF CANADA, Ottawa, Canada. An outstanding exhibit of dinosaurs from Cretaceous beds of Alberta.

ROYAL ONTARIO MUSEUM, Toronto, Canada. Excellent collection of dinosaurs from Cretaceous beds of Alberta.

CARNEGIE MUSEUM, Pittsburgh, Pa. An extraordinary series of Jurassic dinosaurs. Also *Tyrannosaurus.*

MUSEUM OF PALEONTOLOGY OF THE UNIVERSITY OF MICHIGAN, Ann Arbor, Mich. A duck-billed dinosaur.

CHICAGO NATURAL HISTORY MUSEUM, Chicago, Ill. Dinosaurs, especially a handsome display of *Gorgosaurus.*

UNIVERSITY OF NEBRASKA MUSEUM, Lincoln, Neb. Mounted *Stegosaurus* skeleton and other fossil reptiles.

COLORADO MUSEUM OF NATURAL HISTORY, Denver, Colo. Dinosaur skeletons, notably *Diplodocus* and *Trachodon.*

UNIVERSITY OF UTAH, GEOLOGICAL MUSEUM, Salt Lake City, Utah. Mounted *Allosaurus* skeleton, dinosaur tracks, bones.

THE CLEVELAND MUSEUM OF NATURAL HISTORY, Cleveland, Ohio. *Brontosaurus.*

THE BRITISH MUSEUM OF NATURAL HISTORY, London, England. *Archaeopteryx* and numerous dinosaur displays.

BIBLIOGRAPHY

Here are some books on paleontology to give you more knowledge about this endless and fascinating subject.

Andrews, Roy Chapman. *All About Dinosaurs.* New York: Random House, Inc. 1953.

Andrews, Roy Chapman. *In the Days of the Dinosaurs.* New York: Random House, Inc. 1959.

Clark, M. *True Book of Dinosaurs.* Chicago: Childrens Press, 1955.

Colbert, Edwin H. *Millions of Years Ago.* New York: Crowell, Collier & Macmillan, Inc. 1958.

Dickinson, Alice. *The First Book of Prehistoric Animals.* New York: Franklin Watts, Inc. 1954.

Matthews, W. *Exploring the World of Fossils.* Chicago: Childrens Press, 1964.

Posin, Daniel Q. *What is a Dinosaur?* Chicago: Benefic Press, 1961.

Ravielli, A. *Rise and Fall of the Dinosaurs.* New York: Parents' Magazine Press, 1963.

Strahler, A. N. *The Story of Our Earth.* New York: Parents' Magazine Press, 1963.

Advanced Books.

Augusta, J., and Burian, Z. *Prehistoric Animals.* London: Spring Books, 1956.

Colbert, Edwin H. *The Dinosaur Book.* New York: published for the American Museum of Natural History, McGraw-Hill Book Company, 1951.

Colbert, Edwin H. *Dinosaur.* New York: Man and Nature Publications, The American Museum of Natural History, fifth edition edition, 1958.

Dunkle, David H. *The World of the Dinosaurs.* Washington, D.C., Smithsonian Publication No. 4296, 1957.

Fenton, Carroll Lane and Mildred Adams. *The Fossil Book.* New York: Doubleday, 1958.

Moore, Ruth. *Man, Time and Fossils.* New York: Knopf, 1953.

Scheele, William. *Prehistoric Animals.* New York: World, 1954.

INDEX

4833